"C'mon Ducks!"

"C'mon Ducks!"

by Kay Cooper

Photographs by Alvin E. Staffan

Drawings by Janet P. D'Amato

Julian Messner   New York

Designed by Alex D'Amato

Manufactured in the United States of America

Library of Congress Cataloging in Publication Data

Cooper, Kay.
  "C'mon ducks!"

  Includes index.
  SUMMARY: A nine-year-old girl observes the daily
activities of ducks on a lake behind her home.
  1. Ducks—Juvenile literature. [1. Ducks—Habits
and behavior]   I. Staffan, Alvin E.
II D'Amato, Janet.   III. Title.
QL795.B57C59   598.4′1   77-25089
ISBN 0-671-32905-7

For Jill, Bill, and Brian Doll

Acknowledgments

This book owes its existence to many fine people:

H. David Bohlen, ornithologist, Illinois State Museum, Springfield, for checking the text.

Roger Grizzle and R. Paul Sommer who turned over their New Berlin farm to the photographer for duck hatching pictures; and Pat Siciliano of Dawson who provided the photographer with a new Henny Penny.

Jean Seward and Joan Matheny of Lincoln Library, Springfield, for their research and encouragement.

Dr. Paul Johnsgard of the University of Nebraska, Lincoln, for his research and prompt answers.

Glenn and Peggy Younkin of Springfield who put up with the ducks.

Editors Lee M. Hoffman and Madelyn Anderson for their assistance and encouragement.

And to the children, Ann and Susie Watt, who are the actual literary models in this story.

Contents

Books by Kay Cooper

"C'MON DUCKS!"
ALL ABOUT GOLDFISH AS PETS
ALL ABOUT RABBITS AS PETS
A CHIPMUNK'S INSIDE-OUTSIDE WORLD

Ann's Introduction

I was nine when the ducks came. My sister Susie was eight. Now I am eleven.

This book is based on my diary of the ducks. My diary was really lots of sheets of paper kept in a big green folder. It was a lot of fun to watch and write about the ducks. The more I wrote, the more I wanted to learn about them.

I showed my diary to my Mom who writes books. My Mom said other kids would like to read my diary and learn about the ducks. I hope you will like reading about them.

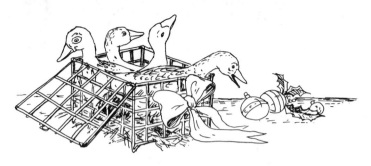

December: Duck Christmas

December 5

Cousin Val, who works at the children's zoo, brought us an early Christmas present today: four ducks. But they are not like any ducks we've ever seen. They are black, white, and red and are called *muscovy ducks*.

I reached down in their wire cage and picked up the largest one. It beat its wings against my hands, and dug its claws into my blue jeans. But I held on, talking softly to it.

The duck opened its beak, making deep breathing noises. It jerked its head back and forth, and wagged its tail from side to side.

Susie, Ann—with duck—and Cousin Val.

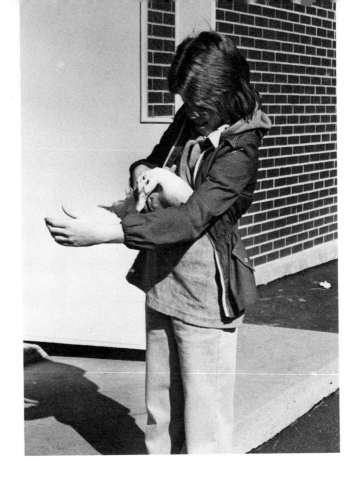

"It's saying hello," explained Val. "Nod and breathe back."

I nodded and breathed. The duck nodded and breathed. I couldn't believe it! I was saying hello to a duck!

I touched the two black feathers above its green eyes, and the snowy white feathers on its body. They felt warm and soft. But the red folds of skin around its beak and eyes felt cold and lumpy.

"This duck is a *white muscovy*," said Val. "I think it's a *drake*, or male, because its so big."

"I like him best," exclaimed my sister Susie. "Let's call him Swimmy."

11

"The others are probably *hens*, or females," Val said. "They are smaller than the drake and are *colored muscovies*." They have white and black feathers and a green color on their backs. Red skin rims their beaks and brown eyes. But they don't all look the same. The biggest has a black body and white neck. We named her Domino. The smallest has white wings. Guess what we call her? Right—White-Wing. And White-Feather has one white feather in the middle of her black tail.

All the muscovies were born in October. They are now six weeks old.

Val is giving two other muscovies named Gus and Gert, to his mother, our Aunt Helen.

White-Wing. . . .

12   **. . . .and White-Feather.**

December 6

      This morning we had a fight over the muscovies. I want to build a pen for them. Susie wants to take them to school for show-and-tell. Mom and Dad think we should let them go. We live on a lake. My parents say that the muscovies will like it there with the other ducks. Maybe they are right.

      In our part of the lake the water never freezes. The power plant near our house uses the lake water to run machines that make electricity for our city. After the water is used, it comes back to the lake at a temperature of 90° Fahrenheit (32° Celsius). This hot water meets the cold lake water and keeps our part of the lake warm.

Power plant on the lake.

These mallards find warm water even in winter.

Wild ducks and other wildlife live in this warm water in winter. Sometimes, hundreds of ducks swim behind our house.

Our muscovies might be best off there. We can still watch them, and bring them food.

Dad finally settles the argument: Susie can take two ducks to school, then, we must let them go. We agree.

December 7

At school Susie and I are together in a split third-and-fourth grade class. Everyone there likes the muscovies. But the muscovies don't like school. White-Wing hides behind Swimmy. Swimmy ruffles up his feathers so he looks big and scary—and stabs at our teacher with his beak.

After school, we let the ducks go. They waddle down

the hill behind our house and jump in the lake. Swimmy leads the hens to the farthest bank.

Now, I'm in bed. Outside, somewhere on the lake, swim our Christmas presents. I feel sad. They probably won't come back. And I can't stop thinking of all the things that can happen to them.

Show-and-tell.

Two dogs along the shore don't look friendly!

They'll have to watch out for muskrats, raccoons, dogs, and kids who throw rocks. And then there are some people who like muscovy duck dinners. Ugh! I could never eat a muscovy duck.

I wonder if our muscovies will live 15 years. Val says that is about how long a muscovy can live. But not many do—not with all those enemies.

December 8

The muscovies—all four of them—are still on the lake!

I called, "C'mon Ducks!" real loud. And Swimmy came, running up the hill, beating his wings against the earth. He wagged his tail, nodded, and breathed to say hello. I said hello too, and offered him some corn kernels from my hand. Swimmy buried his beak in my hand and ate all the corn.

The hens came too, and ate from my hand. Then, the ducks waddled back to the lake.

16

Now every time we go out to see the ducks, we call them to us—"C'mon ducks!"

Domino, Swimmy, White-Feather, and Gert coming to feed.

White-Feather first!

Mallards—the female swimming behind the male.

December 16

It's been ten days since our muscovies came. Susie and I have a feeding station, a round piece of concrete, for them. They love mashed apples and tomatoes along with their bread and corn.

The muscovies bring their friends to eat with them. Today I counted 128 *mallards*, one male *pintail*, and one male *American wigeon*. They eat a lot of food!

The male mallard, with his green head, white collar, and brown breast is easier to identify than his plain brown and white mate.

Susie thinks the male wigeon is the prettiest duck. His white patches shine against his dark body. The wigeon always sits with his back to the feeding station. After all the ducks have left, he walks down to the station and pokes around the con-

An American male wigeon. He's also called a baldpate. He does look bald on top, but he's not—those are white feathers.

A male pintail.

crete for left-overs. We guess this particular duck doesn't like crowds. Most wigeons like company. They like to make friends with pintails, especially.

We like the male pintail a lot. He whistles softly to us, and eats corn from our hands. But, we worry about him. He seems too thin, and something is wrong with his leg. He limps.

December 20

The lake breathed today. I saw its breath just like I see my warm breath in the cold air. The warm lake water and the cold air make layers of mist.

Our muscovies are almost lost in the lake's breath.

A male wood duck . . . . and the female.

December 23

Christmas vacation at last.

Mom and I put old tree branches along the shoreline. Mom thinks the branches will provide cover for the muscovies.

The muscovies swim around the branches. Domino rests her breast on a branch, pulls her legs into her feathers, and sleeps.

December 25

Christmas! Mom and Dad gave us binoculars and three books on ducks. Now Susie and I can really watch the ducks, and learn more about them, too.

One book tells about the senses of a duck. Ducks have the same senses people have. They can smell, see, taste, feel, and hear.

A duck's ears are behind its eyes like ours—but hidden by feathers.

Because a duck's eyes are on the sides of its head, it sees a different picture with each eye.

I'd love to have a duck's eyes. A duck can see a lot farther than I can. It can pick out its mate 200 yards away among hundreds of ducks. That's like me seeing Susie almost one mile away and being able to pick her out among all the kids at school! A duck sees colors, too, just like we do.

The book tells us that wild ducks are *dabblers* or *puddlers*. We laugh at the names, but they're called that because of the way ducks search for food. They make little, quick movements with their bills and stretch their necks down into the water and their tails tip up into the air. It's fun watching ducks dabble!

Dabbling.

December 26

Another of our new books tells about muscovies. All *domestic*, or tame, ducks except the muscovy come from the wild mallard duck. Muscovies come from the wild muscovies that still live along the rivers and streams of Central and South America. They roost in trees and lay their eggs in tree holes.

In 1514, Spanish explorers found the Muisca Indians of Colombia raising huge ducks to eat. Drakes weigh about 12 pounds (5.4 kg.); hens about ten pounds (4.5 kg.). The explorers took some of these ducks home to Spain and called them "Muiscas" after the Indians who raised them. Soon, the word "Muiscas" became "muscovy."

December 29

Susie and I have decided to keep a record of the kinds of ducks that come to the feeding station, and how many there are. We write it down in a notebook along with the temperature and weather conditions for the day.

Today we wrote: "Dec. 29. At the feeding station we saw our four muscovies, 2 wood ducks, about 160 mallards, and two wigeons. The temperature is 6 below 0, and sometimes it starts to spit snow. Also, we just noticed the male pintail. His leg seems better."

We are especially proud of the *wood ducks*. They are the only pair on the lake and they decided to live in our backyard. We made a shelter for them along the shoreline. It's cozy and warm. Straw and oak leaves are piled high inside a large rock crevice. Oak and evergreen branches hide the entrance.

Wood ducks are small—about half the size of a mallard. But the female has a big, frightening voice! When we first heard her, we expected to see an eagle, not a little wood duck. The male's voice is just right for his size—nice and soft.

The male wood duck begs us for food. He wags his tail from side to side and peeps for more. The female watches from a distance. She won't eat until we leave the feeding station. We watch her from inside the house.

December 30

We found that wild ducks act tame when they're hungry. They whine like puppies for food, and eat from our hands just like the muscovies.

I don't worry about the ducks freezing. Their body temperatures are a little warmer than people's—Ours is 98.6° Fahrenheit (37° Celsius), and ducks are about 101° Fahrenheit (38.3° Celsius).

Ducks also have a three-layered blanket to keep them warm. Their skins have a layer of soft, short fuzz. Then,

23

This is how Swimmy's wing feathers look.

there's a layer of soft, fluffy feathers, called down, which covers the lower part of each feather. Their feather cover is thick and stiff.

Ducks also have a thick layer of fat under their skins. Cold air has a hard time getting through fat.

Sometimes, I see ducks swimming with snow on their backs. Snow and water don't dampen feathers. Each feather has a little oil in it to keep it dry. Most of the oil comes from a preen gland on the duck's back near the tail. It looks like a tiny pink pocket. When *preening*, or grooming, a duck rubs its beak against the pocket until oil comes out and coats its beak. Then the duck rubs the oil on the feathers needing it most.

And this is one of Swimmy's sharp, strong claws with webbing in between.

anuary: A New Arrival

January 4

Bad news! Aunt Helen called to say that her muscovies are sick and can't walk. She has been keeping them in the backyard and feeding them only corn.

I tell her our books say she can cure the muscovies by feeding them differently. The best foods for ducks are shelled corn, and mixtures of ground grains that have vitamins, salt, soybeans, wheat, and other things in them. We buy these foods at Mr. Claus's feed store.

r. Claus and Susie
ading a 50-pound
sack of food for
hungry ducks.

January 12

Good news! Gus and Gert are all well again.

January 14

More bad news! Gus has been killed by a dog. Aunt Helen's backyard is no place for ducks. She is bringing Gert to us in the morning.

January 15

Gert has arrived. And now there's trouble—our muscovies don't like her!

Perhaps it's Gert's fault. She really acts strange! First, she waddles up to our muscovies and grumbles. Our muscovies just stare at her. Gert grumbles louder and louder. Then, she marches to the rocks that edge the lake. Unfolding her black and white wings, she hops on a rock and sits facing the water.

Our muscovies chatter among themselves. Then, Domino leaves the group. She swims over to Gert. Reaching up with her long neck, Domino locks her beak around Gert's throat and pulls. Gert tumbles into the water with Domino standing on her back.

I scream at Domino. But Domino hits Gert on the head with her beak. Gert cries out, and beats her wings against the water. I scream again, and Domino digs her claws into Gert's back. Gert shrieks, churns her wings wildly, and finally breaks free. Beating her way across the water, Gert disappears.

This Is Gert.

January 17

Glenn, our next door neighbor, told me that he saw our muscovies chasing Gert through the woods.

"They didn't look too friendly," Glenn said. "And Gert was crying."

January 18

Gert didn't come to the feeding station today. Perhaps she is on her way back to Aunt Helen's. Mom called Aunt Helen in case Gert tries to cross the lake. But the rest of the lake is frozen—only our part of the lake flows. Gert will have a terrible time crossing the ice. I wish she were here!

January 23

I think I've figured out Gert. According to one of our duck books, Gert threatened our hens.

Gert was even bigger than Domino, the largest of our hens. The largest hen is usually the oldest. And the oldest is the boss! This arrangement—with the oldest ruling the youngest—is called a *pecking order*.

When Gert came, she saw that she was the largest hen and should be the boss. Domino saw it too and didn't want Gert to take her place. So, Domino chased Gert away.

February: Swimmy

February 3

Swimmy is gone! I've looked for him all over the lake, calling and calling. I found some white feathers scattered along the rocks. And in the mud I found the footprints of a raccoon! Could there have been a fight?

I feel terrible. The lake will never be the same. Now there's no white duck to say hello to.

February 6

Guess who brought me a muscovy? Dad! A man brought it to Dad's store in a garbage can.

It's a large and very unfriendly drake that likes to stab little kids—like me. I let him go. I didn't even want to name him.

He made friends with Domino. They swam together. But the other hens stayed away from him. I wonder why.

February 8

The new drake disappeared today. Hurray!

February 12

Swimmy is alive—and back home!

I found him sitting in a tree in the backyard. I called him and he flew down for a landing right at my feet.

"Hello, Swimmy," I said. "Where have you been?"

Swimmy said hello and made gurgling noises deep in his throat.

I knelt down to pat him just as Susie came running with bread. She held out the bread to Swimmy, and he snapped it from her fingers.

Swimmy at 6 weeks . . .

As Swimmy leaned over to eat I noticed a red spot on the back of his neck. The red was his skin. I guess the raccoon had ripped out the feathers there. I noticed other changes too. Swimmy was bigger. His body was wider. The red skin on his face had grown thicker and covered the black feathers above his eyes. It's amazing how much a duck can change in just nine days.

. . . and Swimmy grown up.

March: Gert Makes New Friends

March 10

Now Gert has come back. She's in the backyard squeaking at Swimmy. But when Domino comes along, Gert moves away and sits alone on the rocks. Perhaps Gert has accepted a lower place in the pecking order and will let Domino rule.

March 15

Susie has a pet of her own, a chicken called Henny Penny. Henny Penny is white with a red crown. And she's already laid an egg for Susie's breakfast.

Ann and Susie with Henny Penny.

March 20

Today, Susie found Henny Penny asleep with Gert under a tree.

Gert prefers Henny Penny to our muscovies and even seems to "talk" to her. Henny Penny "listens," cocking her head from side to side. Sometimes, Henny Penny follows Gert to the lake and sits on a rock to watch Gert take a bath.

Gert takes the funniest bath I've ever seen. She runs across the water, dives, pops up, and beats her wings until the water flies high in all directions. The other muscovies just splash.

Gert is also a comic eater. She races through the grass to stir up insects, then snaps them up as they fly in front of her!

March 22

Gert has another friend—my grandfather.

Everytime Granddaddy Jack comes to our house he asks, "Where's my Gert?" He walks around the backyard, calling "Gert!" He has bread for her and sometimes a few kernels of corn.

Gert flies in from the lake and walks over to Granddaddy Jack. Then Gert bows to him. And he bows to Gert!

March 24

Gert did a strange thing today. She walked around a large oak tree and lifted her head toward its branches. Clapping the upper and lower parts of her beak together, she made rattling noises. She lowered her head, stepped back, and bowed to the tree.

She circled the tree three times, rattling and bowing. Then she walked to another oak and did the same thing.

I've looked in all our books for an explanation, but can't find one. Maybe Gert is looking for a tree hole to make a nest, or a place to perch. The ducks like to perch up high. Sometimes they come to our bedroom windows and perch, talking to us. It sounds like "hmm hmm" or "huh huh huh." All of them sound a little different—just like people.

April: Baby Mallards

April 3

Guess what? I've discovered a mallard nest in a clump of violets along the lake. There are 11 eggs, all light green. The nest is lined with fluffy down that the mother duck has pulled from her own breast.

A mallard is sitting on her nest. The arrow points to the down with which it is lined.

April 23

Eleven baby mallards! Nine are yellow and brown; two are all yellow.

We've a special food for them that Mr. Claus gave us. It's a mixture of grain, all ground up for baby ducks.

Susie and I pour the food on the feeding station and yell, "C'mon Ducks!" The mother understands and leads the babies to the station. I can hardly wait to see the babies up close.

The mother walks right up to us with her babies following. I want to reach down and hold one, but I don't. They would be afraid. I stand still and talk softly to them. One pecks at my bedroom slippers. It must really be hungry!

The mother is light brown—not as dark as most female mallards. Susie names her "Mary Mallard."

Mary Mallard waits until all her babies have eaten before she eats. She also waits until all her babies are with her before taking off again. Mary Mallard is a good mother.

Mary Mallard with five of her babies.

Baby ducks have many enemies, like turtles and largemouth bass that live in the lake.

The water of the lake is dangerous too. The wind may stir up rough waves, which sweep the ducks away from their mother. They get lost. Some are crushed against rocks. Others are swept between the rocks. Too small to climb, the baby ducks starve.

I think of all these dangers and worry. But—all of Mary Mallard's babies survive the day.

April 25

Today another mallard appeared with seven babies. And she left them in our backyard and took off! The poor babies ran in circles, peeping and searching for their mother.

I waited. In about 30 minutes, the mother came back for her flock. This time I recognized her as the duck we call "Loudy." She has the loudest "quack!" of any mallard.

Nestling ducks.

April 26

This morning Susie and I watched Loudy lead four babies across the lake. The other three are gone—maybe a raccoon got them.

The drakes saw Loudy, too. They flew into the flock to get to her and killed one baby. The dead duck, its neck broken, bobbed in the water. The other ducks kept swimming. We felt bad. We caught the dead duck in a fish net and buried it in the woods.

April 27

Now Loudy has really done it! She left her babies in our yard again. They peeped for a while, but now they are quiet. Huddled together on a rock, they are waiting for their mother. Loudy's not a very good mother.

April 28

It's a lucky day for Loudy's ducks. Mary Mallard, who has not lost one baby, has adopted Loudy's ducks. She gathers all 14 around her.

April 29

Help! Two men in a motor boat zigzag across the lake, heading for Mary Mallard and her ducks. Mary Mallard screeches and races away, with the little ducks following. But they're too slow. The racing boat slams into them. Five babies are dead. Mary Mallard is hurt. Her left wing and foot hang to the side.

Laughing, the men head their boat for another part of the lake. As soon as it is out of sight, Mary Mallard moves to the head of the flock. She leads the babies that are left to the farthest bank, and disappears.

April 30

Mary Mallard brings her ducks to the feeding station today. Her wing looks better, but her foot is swollen and black. Dad says she may lose her toes.

Mary Mallard.

Dad brought medicine to help Mary Mallard's foot get better. The trick is giving it to her—it's a pill. Dad suggests that I wrap the pill in a small piece of bread, get Mary Mallard alone, and throw her the bread.

We tried it. While Susie called Mary Mallard's babies to her for feeding, I called Mary. She came to me and I threw her the bread. She took it! Was I surprised! Now, Mary Mallard's foot will get better.

May: Egg Watch

May 8

Gert has a nest on the rocks under the shade of an oak tree. It's covered with dried oak leaves. I push away the leaves with a stick to see her egg. It's beautiful—about two inches long and light yellow. I push the leaves back. I hope Gert doesn't know I was here.

May 9

White-Wing has laid an egg. It's in Gert's nest.

May 10

Now White-Feather has an egg. It's in Gert's nest too!

May 11

Domino has an egg—in Gert's nest. What will happen when all the muscovies try to sit on Gert's nest at the same time?

May 21

There's no doubt about who will be sitting on the nest. Domino! I should have known. Domino rules the hens.

Susie made the mistake of walking up to the nest. Domino hissed and snapped at Susie. Now, we can't count the eggs.

Our books say that one hen can raise 30 ducklings a year. She usually makes two nests—one in the spring and one in the fall. We may have too many baby ducks!

May 23

I can't stand it! It's so hot that White-Feather and White-Wing are fainting! They've made a new nest in the sun on our neighbor Glenn's beach. This afternoon they stood over their eggs and fanned them with their tails. They panted.

Beads of water rolled off their tongues. Their eyes closed. Their heads dropped and they collapsed on the nest.

Finally, I got those ducks some shade. I put the umbrella for our picnic table over their nest. Were they scared! They raced away. I ran after them.

I caught White-Wing and placed her on the nest. I talked to her and patted her head. She stayed. Then, I caught White-Feather and she messed all over me. Ugh! Did I stink!

Mom made me wash outside and take off my clothes in the garage. Then, I took a shower. When I dressed, I walked outside to look at the nest.

Under the umbrella sat White-Wing, snuggled next to White-Feather, snuggled next to Swimmy! Everyone was squeaking.

May 25

The muscovies leave their nests only once during the day to feed and bathe. I think it must be very boring.

This afternoon I sat under the umbrella with the ducks and read them a story. Swimmy sat close by, watching and listening. I guess they don't understand me, but like the sound of my voice.

May 26

   Mr. Kent, our neighbor, called and is very upset. Gert has built another nest—under the seat of his pontoon boat. She has attacked Mr. Kent's dogs, and has chased Mr. Kent off the boat.

   We went to Mr. Kent's, and looked into a dark hole under the seat. There sat Gert, looking back at us. Mom laughed. But Mr. Kent didn't think it was so funny. "I want that duck off my boat right now!" he roared.

   Mom picked up Gert and carried her home. Susie and I gathered up the eggs—14 in all. We slipped Gert's eggs under White-Wing and White-Feather and hoped they'd hatch. Muscovy eggs take about 35 days to hatch—that's a long time to wait.

May 30

   Bad news! This morning I went to White-Feather and White-Wing's nest. Feathers, eggs, and down were scattered all over the place. White-Wing was gone. White-Feather was sitting on two eggs in a clump of down.

   Raccoons? I searched the beach for animal tracks, but didn't find any. I searched the shoreline and called.

   All day I kept going back to the nest to see if White-Wing was there. She wasn't. I know White-Wing is dead. If she were alive, she'd be sitting on that nest. I feel terrible!

Summertime: Sad Endings

June 3

School is over. Great! Now Susie and I can spend more time with the ducks and find out more about them.

We discovered where Swimmy and Gert sleep at night. Unfortunately, it's on Mr. Kent's boat dock.

Ducks sleep with their heads bent over their backs and their beaks buried in their feathers.

Swimmy is sleeping—with half an eye open.

Some of the mallards sleep floating in the water. Others rest along the shore. Why did Swimmy and Gert have to pick Mr. Kent's boat dock?

The mallards aren't quiet at night. They quack and quack.

June 16

Domino has been sitting on her nest for 35 days and her eggs haven't hatched. Instead, they've turned black. I crack one open to see what's happening inside. Smelly, green stuff comes out. Ick! Does it stink!

Susie cracks one egg from White-Feather's nest. Ugh!

The eggs are infertile—they cannot produce baby ducks. Maybe the hens are too young. Their bodies aren't yet ready to make fertile eggs—eggs that can produce baby ducks.

Cousin Val says that we must tear up the nests. Otherwise, the hens will sit on them for months, become weak, and may die.

We wait until the ducks leave to eat. We gather up the eggs and nests. We dump everything in the woods.

When we return, Domino is sitting on the spot where her nest used to be. White-Feather is on the beach, turning over twigs with her beak. Now, we have two sad and confused ducks.

46

But, in a few minutes, they are off and swimming.

July 1

Now Gert has made a third nest. But she picked a bad place. It's where White-Wing and White-Feather nested.

There, on the beach, Gert is at the mercy of whatever killed White-Wing. And her eggs may be infertile. We talk over the problem with Mom and Dad. The only thing we can do is tear up the nest and put Gert's eggs in an incubator.

July 2

Today Dad rented a chicken incubator. A *chicken incubator* is a special cabinet which warms eggs and keeps them warm so they can hatch.

Here's how Susie and I work it: We always keep the tray in the bottom of the incubator filled with warm water. Duck eggs need lots of moisture. We spray the eggs with warm water twice a day. We use a bottle with a push-spray top. Before filling the bottle, we make sure there's no stale, cool water trapped in the nozzle hose. We take off the sprayer from the bottle and push the button until no more water comes out.

Two times a day we turn the eggs. We keep a "turning record" by marking the eggs with the letter "G" for Gert. At breakfast, all the Gs face up. At dinner, the Gs face down.

We're careful to check that the switch for the fan and heating rod is always turned on. We check the thermometer too. It should read between 101° and 103° Fahrenheit (38.3°-39° Celsius).

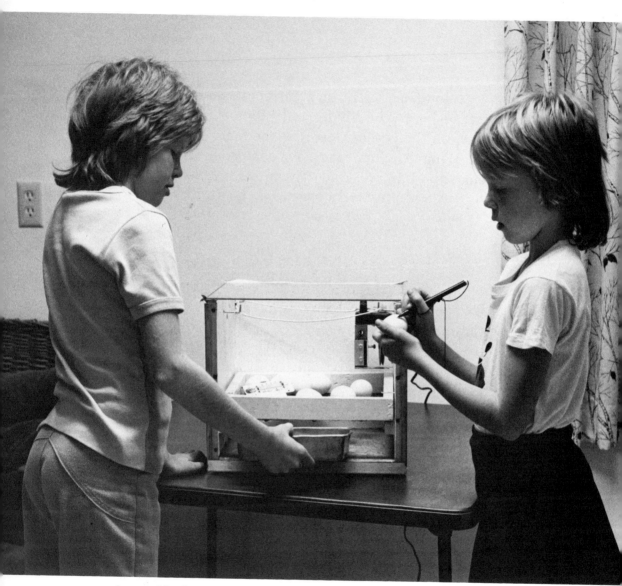

Ann and Susie are marking eggs in the incubator.

July 9

Tonight we *candled*, or examined, Gert's eggs to see if they were fertile. You can see blood spots and veins inside a fertile egg. Later, you can see the baby duck moving inside the egg and hear it pecking the shell to get out.

We darkened the living room and turned on Dad's slide projector. It has a very bright light. Susie held up one egg about two feet in front of the projector light. We looked through the shell. Nothing. The egg was clear—it was infertile. All of Gert's eggs were infertile!

July 29.

Another bad problem. Mr. Kent called again. This time, White-Feather has a nest under the seat of the pontoon. And Mr. Kent threw all the eggs in the lake. Mr. Kent wants us to clean up the mess White-Feather has made under the seat.

Some people don't think ducks are very important.

July 31

Today was very sad. Henny Penny was killed by Mr. Kent's dogs. Mom buried Henny Penny in the woods. Poor Susie. Poor Gert.

49

August 2

I think Domino has a nest. She comes to the feeding station just before dark, eats a bite of food, takes a bath, and flies away.

August 3

Today I followed Domino. I waited until she was taking a bath before I walked to the place where I had last seen her.

Swimmy is mating Domino.

I waited twenty minutes. I didn't know that ducks took such long baths.

Finally, she came, flying low over the water. She landed on some rocks and hopped behind a tree. I followed. Beneath the tree was her nest. Maybe these eggs are fertile. I certainly hope so.

September 1

I'm a grandmother! Domino has one baby duck—and is it cute. Susie calls him—or her—"Checkers." It's bright yellow, almost orange. But it will be all white, like Swimmy, when it's grown. Swimmy is Checkers' father. If Checkers were brown and yellow, it would grow up to be black and white, like Domino.

The baby duck follows Domino everywhere, staying right behind her tail. It peeps and peeps. But Domino doesn't have a loud voice—muscovies don't quack. If Checkers should wander too far away and become lost, Domino couldn't call it to her. She would just wait for Checkers to come back.

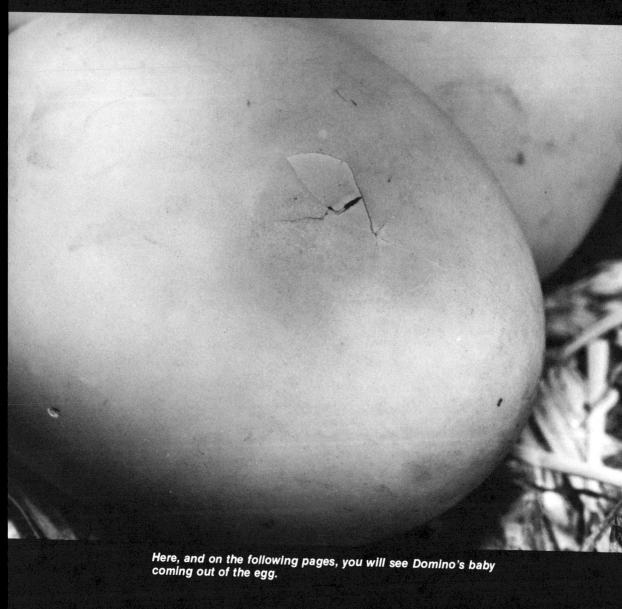

Here, and on the following pages, you will see Domino's baby coming out of the egg.

52

September 3

Domino won't let anyone near her baby. Susie got too close today and was attacked! Domino hissed, spread out her wings, and tail feathers, and flew into Susie's knees.

Our books say that muscovies are one of the most protective ducks.

September 12

Checkers is gone! We don't know what happened. Domino is swimming with our other muscovies and there is no Checkers. We feel awful.

September 15

School again. And our muscovies look terrible. Their feathers are falling off and new ones are coming in. This is called *molting*. Old feathers wear and break off. Birds need a new set of feathers each year so they can keep their bodies warm, and keep flying.

September 16

We're worried that the ducks won't have enough water to swim in. There hasn't been any rain for weeks and the lake water is down almost five feet. There's hardly any water at all in our part of the lake. Our muscovies have moved over to the main part of the lake where there's more water.

September 27

   Swimmy, Domino, Gert, and White-Feather don't come to the feeding station anymore. They are still over in the main part of the lake. We feel very sad they aren't here.
   Susie and I still feed the mallards and call, "C'mon Ducks!"

Mary Mallard comes. She has lost all her toes because of those men in the motor boat. She walks on the back of her foot.

Mary Mallard's babies come. Loudy comes to the feeding station. And about 15 other mallards, and a male pintail.

But our muscovies don't come. We sure do miss them.

I've read the muscovies sometimes become wild and stay away from people. I sure hope ours don't. I sure wish they would come back. Maybe, some day.

Glossary

CANDLE: to examine the inside of an egg by holding it in front of a light

DABBLERS: the name given to wild ducks because of the way they search the water for food.

DOMESTIC: tame

DOWN: fine, soft, fluffy feathers of a young duck. Down also covers the lower part of each feather of an adult bird

DRAKE: a male duck

DUCKLING: a young duck

FERTILE EGGS: eggs that can produce ducklings

HEN: a female duck

INCUBATOR: a special cabinet which warms fertile eggs so they can hatch

INFERTILE EGGS: eggs that cannot produce ducklings

MALLARD: a wild duck. The male has a green head and neck. The female is brown and white

MOLTING: the shedding of feathers

MUSCOVY: a duck found wild in Central and South America, but domesticated, or tamed, around the world. It is often black and white with red folds of skin on its face

PECKING ORDER: an arrangement within a group of ducks in which the stronger or oldest duck rules the weaker or younger duck

PINTAIL: a wild duck with brown, gray, and white feathers and a pointed tail

PREEN: to smooth or clean feathers with the beak

PREEN GLAND: a gland just over the duck's tail from which oil comes. The oil helps to keep the duck's feathers dry

PUDDLERS: *See* DABBLERS

WIGEON: a wild duck with brown, gray, white, and green feathers. The male has a white crown

WOOD DUCK: a wild duck with a crest on its head. The male is blue, purple, red, brown, and white. The female is brown-gray with a white eye patch

Index